SCHOLASTIC

TIMES TABLES

PRACTICE BOOK

AGES 5–7

$2 \times 6 = 12$

$5 \times 3 = 15$

$10 \times 8 = 80$

Be a times tables master

Scholastic Education, an imprint of Scholastic Ltd
Book End, Range Road, Witney, Oxfordshire, OX29 0YD
Registered office: Westfield Road, Southam, Warwickshire CV47 0RA
www.scholastic.co.uk

© 2018, Scholastic Ltd
1 2 3 4 5 6 7 8 9   8 9 0 1 2 3 4 5 6 7

British Library Cataloguing-in-Publication Data
A catalogue record for this book is available from the British Library.
ISBN 978-1407-18244-5
Printed and bound by Bell & Bain

Due to the nature of the web we cannot guarantee the content or links of any site mentioned.
We strongly recommend that teachers check websites before using them in the classroom.

Every effort has been made to trace copyright holders for the works reproduced in this book, and the publishers apologise for any inadvertent omissions.

Author
Louise Carruthers
Editorial
Rachel Morgan, Shannon Keenlyside, Audrey Stokes, Helen Lewis and Gemma Smith
Cover and Series Design
Scholastic Design Team: Nicolle Thomas, Neil Salt and Alice Duggan
Illustration
Gaynor Barrs

Contents

How to use this book

Rapid recall of the 2, 5 and 10 times tables by the end of Year 2 and all other times tables facts up to 12 × 12 by the end of Year 4 is a key expectation for all children in England. In fact, so key that all children will sit a Times Tables Check at the end of Year 4 from 2020.

Why are the times tables important?

They support mathematical learning and understanding. If you know your times tables, this frees up space to learn and work on new mathematical concepts and problems. And, as you know, we use them all the time in daily life, for example, when working out costs, doubling recipes and finding out how much we will need of something (for example, *we need to put 6 chairs at each of the 8 tables. 8 × 6 = 48, so we'll need 48 chairs*).

How does *Times Tables* help children master multiplication?

This *Practice Book* aims to give children the chance to practise their times tables, deepening their understanding as well as increasing their rapid recall. This means they understand the 'how and why' of multiplication as well as being able to answer multiplication facts quickly. They will understand, for example:

▶ You can multiply two numbers in any order and the answer will be the same:
If you know 2 × 5 = 10, then you also know 5 × 2 = 10.

▶ You can break up a multiplication fact:
Don't remember 6 × 4? What if you think about it as 4 × 4 + 2 × 4?

▶ Multiplication is repeated addition:
7 × 2 = 2 + 2 + 2 + 2 + 2 + 2 + 2
8 × 2 = 2 + 2 + 2 + 2 + 2 + 2 + 2 + 2
This means that if you know that 7 × 2 = 14, then 8 × 2 will be two more.

How can you help?

▶ Encourage short bursts of practice. Focus on a couple of tables in the first instance and move on to others once your child is confident.

▶ Talk about the times tables. Encourage them to think about what they know and explain their thinking. You'll have opportunities to do this throughout this *Practice Book* as well.

▶ Look for real-life situations for your child to use the times tables. Seeing how you use what you know or showing off what you already know is a great motivator.

▶ Remind your child that our brains are growing when we make mistakes. Celebrate this growth!

▶ Speed may be important but can also cause many children anxiety. Focus on understanding multiplication and rehearsing the times tables in fun ways. Speed will come in time!

Track your progress online using our *free* Times Tables Check:
www.scholastic.co.uk/timestables

Advice for children

This book is full of practice questions and activities to help you master your times tables.

Each unit focuses on a different topic or times table.

This box helps you review a topic before you get practising.

Work through the questions in order.

Use a separate piece of paper if you need more space.

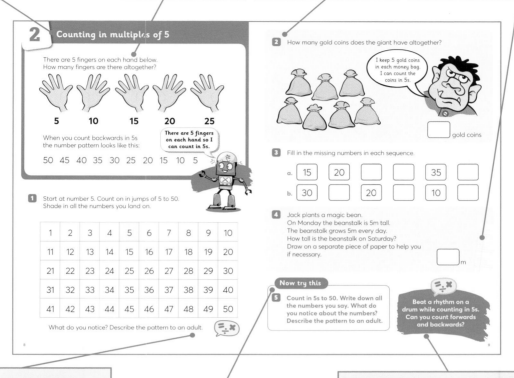

Explaining helps you understand. Be sure to share what you know with a friend or an adult.

Try these questions to extend your learning and deepen understanding.

These fun activities will help you recall your times tables facts outside of the practice book.

Times Tables tips

► Don't rush through the units. Concentrate on one unit at a time. Record your progress using the chart on page 44.

► Celebrate what you already know and think more deeply about it.

► Challenge yourself to master any parts you find tricky. Make your brain grow!

► Use equipment or draw pictures to help you. They are fantastic tools!

► Focus on memorising one or two times tables at a time. Master them, then move on to new ones.

► Times tables speed is great, but understanding is best.

► Look for opportunities to use your times tables every day, for example look at how eggs are arranged in large and small egg boxes and use multiplication to find out how many eggs there are in each box.

► Keep trying. Keep thinking and exploring. You can do it!

Here are some paper clips.

How many do I have?

I will sort them into groups of 2 and count in 2s.

| 2 | 4 | 6 | 8 | 10 | 12 | 14 | 16 |

I have 16 paper clips.

1 **a.** Circle the stars to sort them into groups of 2.
One has been done for you.

b. Count in 2s to find how many.   [ ] stars

6

2 **a.** Complete the pattern and write how many circles.

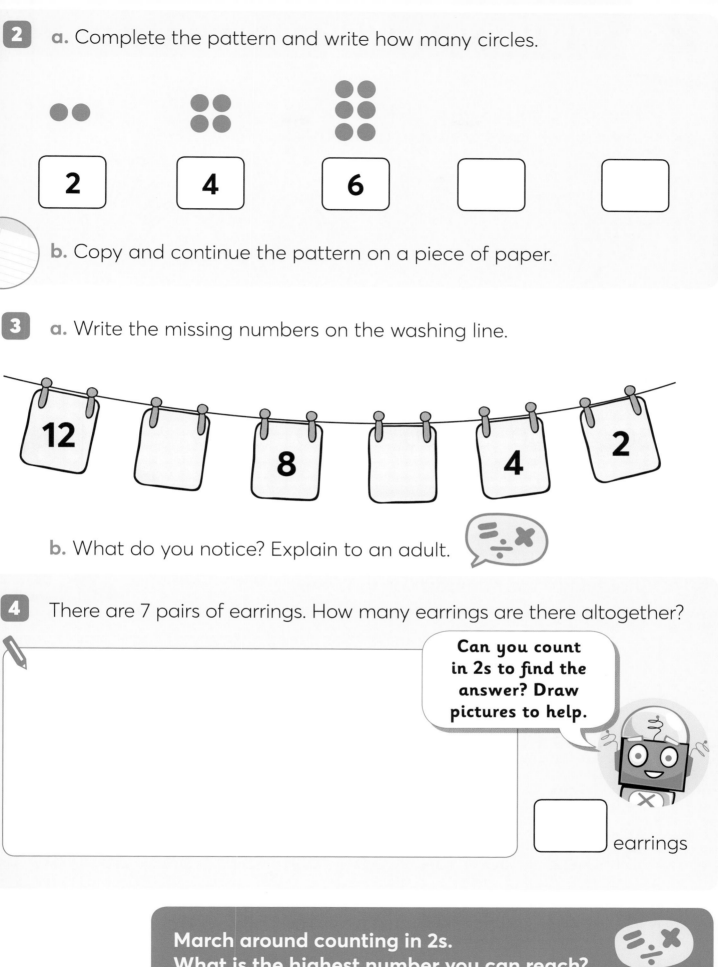

| 2 | 4 | 6 | | |

b. Copy and continue the pattern on a piece of paper.

3 **a.** Write the missing numbers on the washing line.

12   8   4   2

b. What do you notice? Explain to an adult.

4 There are 7 pairs of earrings. How many earrings are there altogether?

Can you count in 2s to find the answer? Draw pictures to help.

earrings

March around counting in 2s.
What is the highest number you can reach?

There are 5 fingers on each hand below.
How many fingers are there altogether?

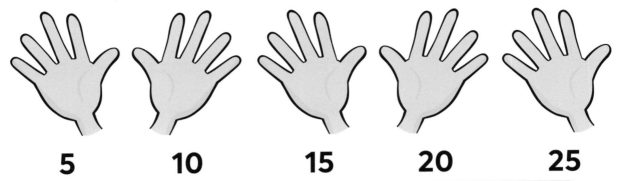

5   **10**   **15**   **20**   **25**

When you count backwards in 5s
the number pattern looks like this:

> There are 5 fingers on each hand so I can count in 5s.

50   45   40   35   30   25   20   15   10   5

1   Start at number 5. Count on in jumps of 5 to 50.
Shade in all the numbers you land on.

1	2	3	4	5	6	7	8	9	10
11	12	13	14	15	16	17	18	19	20
21	22	23	24	25	26	27	28	29	30
31	32	33	34	35	36	37	38	39	40
41	42	43	44	45	46	47	48	49	50

What do you notice? Describe the pattern to an adult.

2 How many gold coins does the giant have altogether?

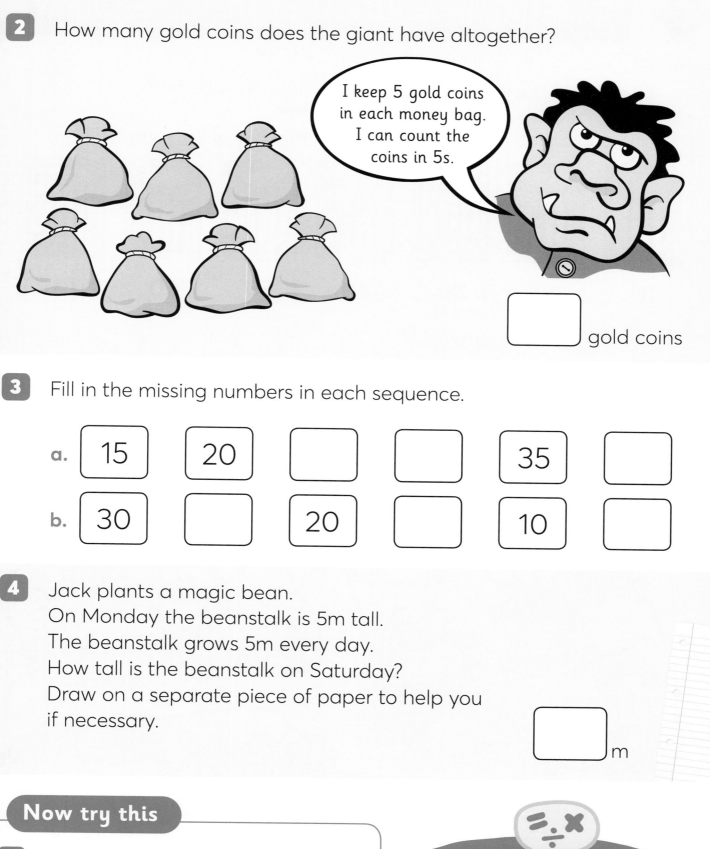

I keep 5 gold coins in each money bag. I can count the coins in 5s.

| | gold coins

3 Fill in the missing numbers in each sequence.

a. | 15 | | 20 | | | | | | 35 | | |

b. | 30 | | | | 20 | | | | 10 | | |

4 Jack plants a magic bean.
On Monday the beanstalk is 5m tall.
The beanstalk grows 5m every day.
How tall is the beanstalk on Saturday?
Draw on a separate piece of paper to help you if necessary.

| |m

Now try this

5 Count in 5s to 50. Write down all the numbers you say. What do you notice about the numbers? Describe the pattern to an adult.

Beat a rhythm on a drum while counting in 5s. Can you count forwards and backwards?

Counting in multiples of 10

Irena has 7 packets of crayons. There are 10 crayons in each packet.
She can count in 10s to find the total number of crayons.

10   **20**   **30**   **40**   **50**   **60**   **70**

Irena has 70 crayons.

1   A crab has 10 legs. How many legs are in each rock pool?
Count in 10s.

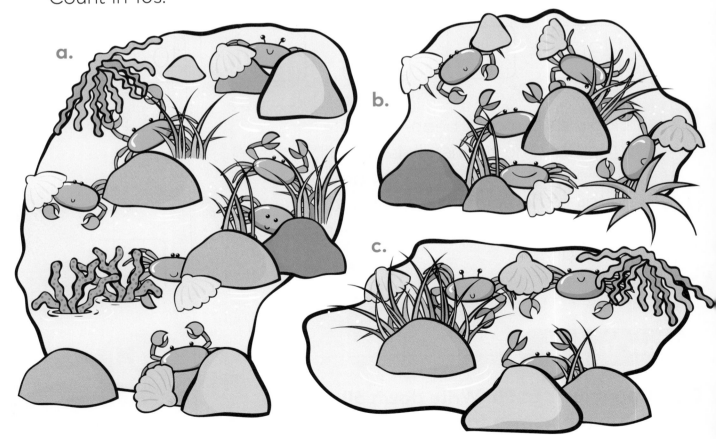

a. _____ legs   b. _____ legs   c. _____ legs

2 Four children are playing hoopla. Each child throws 10 rings. They score 10 points for each ring that lands on the post.

a. Count in 10s to find out how many points each child scores.

Child 1	Child 2	Child 3	Child 4

[ ] points   [ ] points   [ ] points   [ ] points

b. What is the top score that anyone can get? How do you know? Explain to an adult.

3 Fill in the missing numbers.

a. [ ]   [40]   [ ]   [60]   [ ]

b. [100]   [ ]   [80]   [ ]   [ ]

4 Everything in the toy shop costs 10p!

a. Ellie buys 5 toys. How much does she spend? [ ] p

b. Jack buys 8 toys. How much does he spend? [ ] p

Now write your own number story on a piece of paper.

Count in 10s as you throw and catch a ball in the air. How high can you count before you drop the ball? Count in 10s while throwing and catching with a partner. Take turns to say the next number.

Sam is playing a game with two dice. He rolls double 4.

He counts the spots. There are 8 altogether.

Double 4 equals 8. This is the same as 4 + 4 = 8

A double is when a number is added to itself.

1 Colour all the dominoes that show a double.

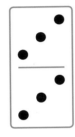   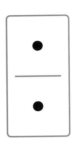 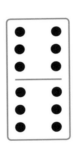 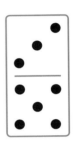

2 Draw the missing spots on the doubles ladybirds.

Join each ladybird to the correct flower.

3 + 3 = 6

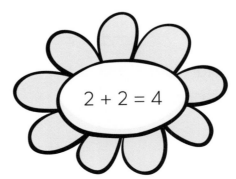

2 + 2 = 4

5 + 5 = 10

3 If a dart lands on the outside ring of the dartboard it scores double points. Fill in the missing doubles in the outside ring. One has been done for you.

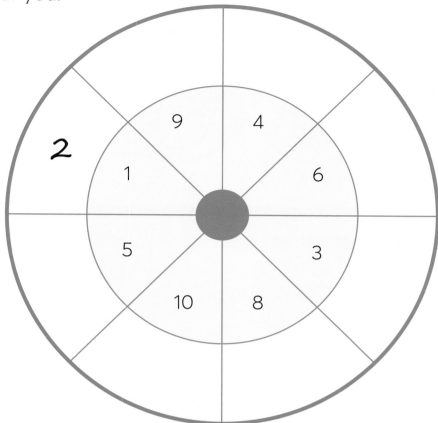

4 **a.** One square has 4 sides. How many sides do 2 squares have?

☐ sides

b. Mila is 8. Joel is double her age. How old is Joel?

☐ years old

Now try this

5 If you double an odd number is your answer an odd number? What if you double an even number? Explain your answer, with examples, to an adult.

 Write 2, 4, 6, 8, 10 and 12 on a piece of paper. Roll two dice. If you roll a double work out the total number of spots on both dice and cross out that number. Continue until you have crossed out every number.

Here are 3 equal groups with 2 cats in each group.

> The 3 tells us the number of equal groups. The 2 tells us how many in each group.

1 The sandwiches have been arranged equally on the plates.

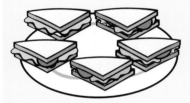  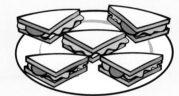 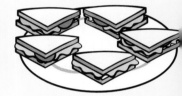

Fill in the numbers in this sentence.

There are ☐ equal groups with ☐ in each group.

2 Draw a line from the group of socks to an equal group of shapes.

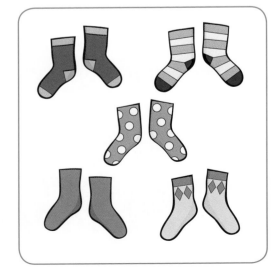

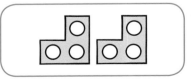

3 Draw equal sets.

   a. Put 5 eggs in each basket.

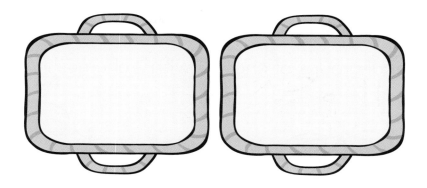

4 Draw a ring around the picture that shows 4 equal groups of 3.

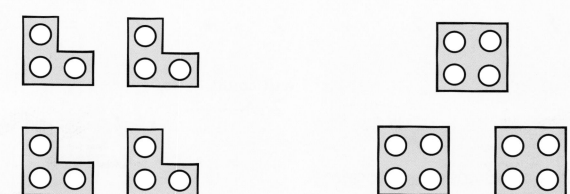

5 **a.** Draw a picture to show 6 equal groups of 2.

b. Draw a picture to show 7 equal groups of 5.

Take a big handful of dried pasta shapes. Can you sort the pasta into equal groups? How many different ways can you sort the pasta into groups?

When we count larger numbers of objects, it helps to count the objects in equal groups.

Here are 4 equal groups of cherries with 2 cherries in each group.

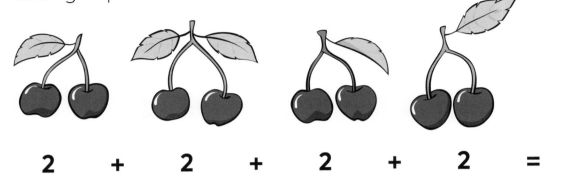

| **2** | **+** | **2** | **+** | **2** | **+** | **2** | **=** | **8** |

I will count in 2s.
2...4...6...8.

There are 8 cherries altogether.

---

1 Join the picture to the correct number sentence.

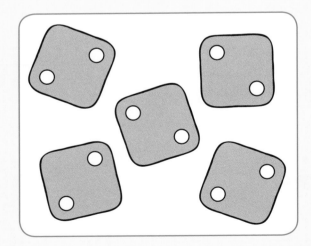

3 + 3 = 6

2 + 2 + 2 + 2 + 2 = 10

5 + 5 = 10

2 Complete the number sentence to show the equal groups.

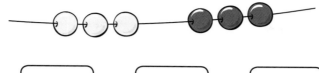

[ ] + [ ] = [ ]

Draw a bead string on a piece of paper to match this number sentence.

$$3 + 3 + 3 + 3 = 12$$

3   **a.** I have 5 packets of seeds.
There are 3 seeds in each packet.
How many seeds do I have altogether?

 seeds

b. Show this as jumps on the number line below.

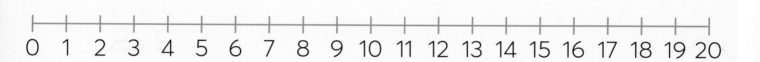

0 1 2 3 4 5 6 7 8 9 10 11 12 13 14 15 16 17 18 19 20

Now try this

4   It is pocket money day.

Would you rather have 8 or 5 ?

Circle your answer.

Explain your ideas to an adult.

 With a 1–6 dice, see how many times you can roll a 5 in a minute.
Keep a tally. Count your tally marks in 5s to find your total score.

row

column

This pattern is called an array.

There are 2 rows of flowers. Each row has 4 flowers. There are 8 flowers altogether.

I can show this as a number sentence: 4 + 4 = 8

There are 4 columns of flowers. Each column has 2 flowers. There are 8 flowers altogether.

I can show this as a number sentence: 2 + 2 + 2 + 2 = 8

 1

a. How many rows of cabbages are there above?

b. How many cabbages are there in each row?

c. How many cabbages are there altogether?

2 Draw arrays to help you solve these problems.

Amelia planted 4 rows of carrots with 2 in each row.

Rory planted 2 rows of carrots with 5 in each row.

Who planted the most carrots? How do you know?

_____

_____

3 4 trees each have 5 apples on them.
How many apples are there altogether?
Draw an array to help you.

[ ] apples

Now try this

4 How many different arrays can you make with 10 counters or coins? Draw arrays on a sheet of paper and describe them to an adult. Do you think you have found them all?

Go on an array hunt around your home or in school. Draw pictures or take photographs of some of the different arrays you find.

How many wheels do 3 bikes have?

2 **4** **6**

We can work out the answer by counting in 2s.

We can add 2 to itself 3 times:

2 + 2 + 2 = 6

The multiplication
3 × 2 = 6 shows that
3 lots of 2 is 6.

We can also use the multiplication sign: ×

This shows that a number has been added to itself a number of times.

1 Write a multiplication to describe the equal groups.

☐ lots of ☐   ☐ × ☐ = ☐

2 Circle the statement that matches the picture.

2 lots of 4   4 lots of 2

3 Draw a picture and write a multiplication to match the story.

8 feet are splashing in the water. How many toes are getting wet?

☐ × ☐ = ☐

4 Write two multiplications to describe this array. What do you notice? Explain to an adult.

☐ × ☐ = ☐

☐ × ☐ = ☐

Make an array using 20 counters. Make another and then another. Write two multiplications for each array.

The 2-times table

If you want to multiply a number by 2 you can count in 2s to work out the answer.

3 × 2 looks like this.

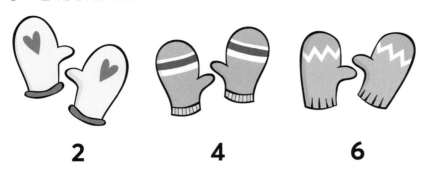

2   **4**   **6**

3 × 2 means 3 lots of 2.

You can count in 2s to find the total: 3 × 2 = 6

---

1 Complete the 2 times table. Use the shoes to help you count. The first one has been done for you.

a. 1 × 2 = __2__	**e.** 5 × 2 = _____	**i.** 9 × 2 = _____
b. 2 × 2 = _____	**f.** 6 × 2 = _____	**j.** 10 × 2 = _____
c. 3 × 2 = _____	**g.** 7 × 2 = _____	**k.** 11 × 2 = _____
d. 4 × 2 = _____	**h.** 8 × 2 = _____	**l.** 12 × 2 = _____

2 **a.** 7 birds each catch 2 worms.

How many worms are caught altogether?

☐ worms

b. 11 birds each lay 2 eggs.

How many eggs are laid altogether?

☐ eggs

3 **a.** Roll two 1–6 dice.

b. Add the two numbers together.

c. Multiply your new number by 2.

d. Colour in the number you have made.

Repeat steps a–d until you have coloured in all the numbers. What do you notice about the numbers?

> Record each step on a piece of paper as you go along.

12	22	8	14
6	12	16	24
4	18	20	10

Now try this

4 Kwame says,

"If you multiply a number by 2, the answer is always even."

Is Kwame correct? Explain your ideas to an adult.

> Can you write the 2-times table in 1 minute? Start from 1 × 2 = 2. Next, start from 12 × 2 and go backwards.

If you want to multiply a number by 5 you can count in 5s to work out the answer. There are 5 petals on each flower below.

4 × 5 looks like this.

5　　**10**　　**15**　　**20**

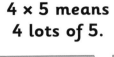

4 × 5 means
4 lots of 5.

You can count in 5s to find the total number of petals.

4 × 5 = 20

1 There are 5 points on each star.
How many points are in each group of stars?

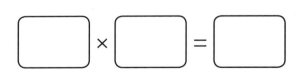

2 There are 5 football stickers in a pack.
Zoe buys 11 packs.
How many stickers does Zoe have altogether?

stickers

3 Fill in the missing numbers on the multiplication wheels.
One has been done for you.

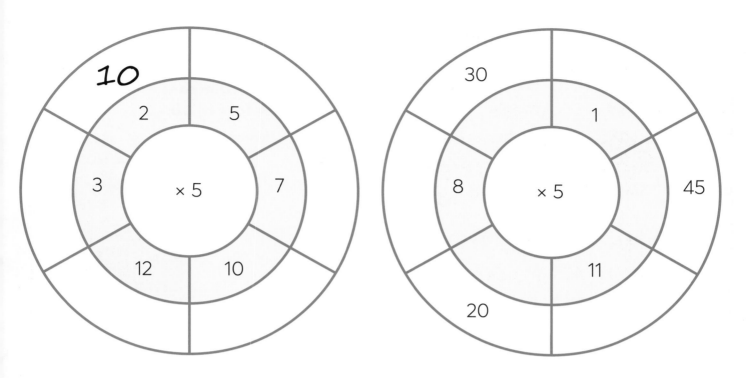

4 Lin needs 5 straws to make the outline of a house shape.

How many straws does she need to build 8 houses?

[   ] straws

Using chalk, write the multiples of 5 to 50 on a pavement or wall. Ask an adult to call out questions from the 5-times table. Work out each answer. Try to hit a ball or beanbag at the correct answer.

Now try this

5 If you multiply a number by 5 the answer will always end in 0.

Is this   **sometimes**   **always**   **never**   correct?

Circle the correct answer. Explain why to an adult.

11 The 10-times table

If you want to multiply a number by 10 you can count in 10s to work out the answer.

4 × 10 looks like this.

10   **20**   **30**   **40**

> 4 × 10 means 4 lots of 10.

You can count in 10s to find the total.

4 × 10 = 40

The 10-times table doubles the 5-times table.

4 × 10 = double 4 × 5

---

1 Multiply each number in the first column by 10.

Draw a line to match it to the correct number in the second column. One has been done for you.

2		110
11		30
7		40
4		20
3		70

2 Use the coins to help you solve the missing number problems.

a. [ ] × 10 = 40   **b.** [ ] × 10 = 60   **c.** [ ] × 10 = 110

3 Mr Green plants 7 rows of potatoes.

He puts 10 potatoes in each row.

How many potatoes does he plant altogether?   [ ] potatoes

4 Balloons come in packs of 10.

a. How many packs do you need to give 44 children a balloon each?   [ ] packs

b. How many balloons are left over? How do you know? Explain to an adult.    [ ] balloons

Set up a 10p shop. Price each item for sale as a multiple of 10p. Your customers can only pay with 10p coins. Make sure you check their money carefully!

I can see that
6 × 5 = 30!

This multiplication table shows the number facts for the 2-, 5- and 10-times tables.

×	0	1	2	3	4	5	6	7	8	9	10	11	12
2	0	2	4	6	8	10	12	14	16	18	20	22	24
5	0	5	10	15	20	25	(30)	35	40	45	50	55	60
10	0	10	20	30	40	50	60	70	80	90	100	110	120

Try to learn these number facts from memory.

1

a. How much do 6 bouncy balls cost?  p

b. How much do 7 pots of bubbles cost?  p

c. How much do 10 water bombs cost?  p

2 Join the multiplications that have the same total.
One has been done for you.

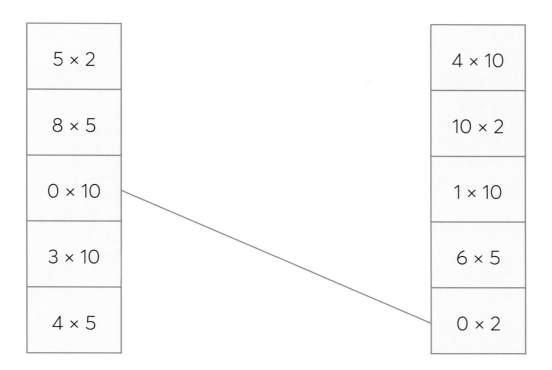

5 × 2
8 × 5
0 × 10
3 × 10
4 × 5

4 × 10
10 × 2
1 × 10
6 × 5
0 × 2

3 Fill in the missing numbers.

a. 8 × 10 = ☐

c. 1 × 10 = ☐

e. ☐ × 10 = 70

b. ☐ × 10 = 50

d. ☐ × 10 = 90

f. 12 × 10 = ☐

Now try this

4 The total is 20.
What is the multiplication?
Write down all the answers you can think of.

Draw a hopscotch grid using chalk. Write a multiplication from the 2-, 5- or 10-times table in each section. Throw a stone. Answer the multiplication in that section. Hop across the grid to collect the stone and have another go.

Colour in to win!

This is a game for 2 players.

You will need:

a 1–6 dice
coloured crayons for each player

- Take turns to roll the dice.

- Multiply your dice number by 2, 5 or 10.

- Colour the answer on the board with your coloured crayon.

- Continue to play, in turns, until all the numbers have been coloured.

- The winner is the player with the most coloured sections on the grid.

Use counters instead of crayons if you want to play the game again!

2	10	15	30	5
12	4	20	2	10
25	30	5	50	6
40	15	20	6	2
4	60	12	60	8

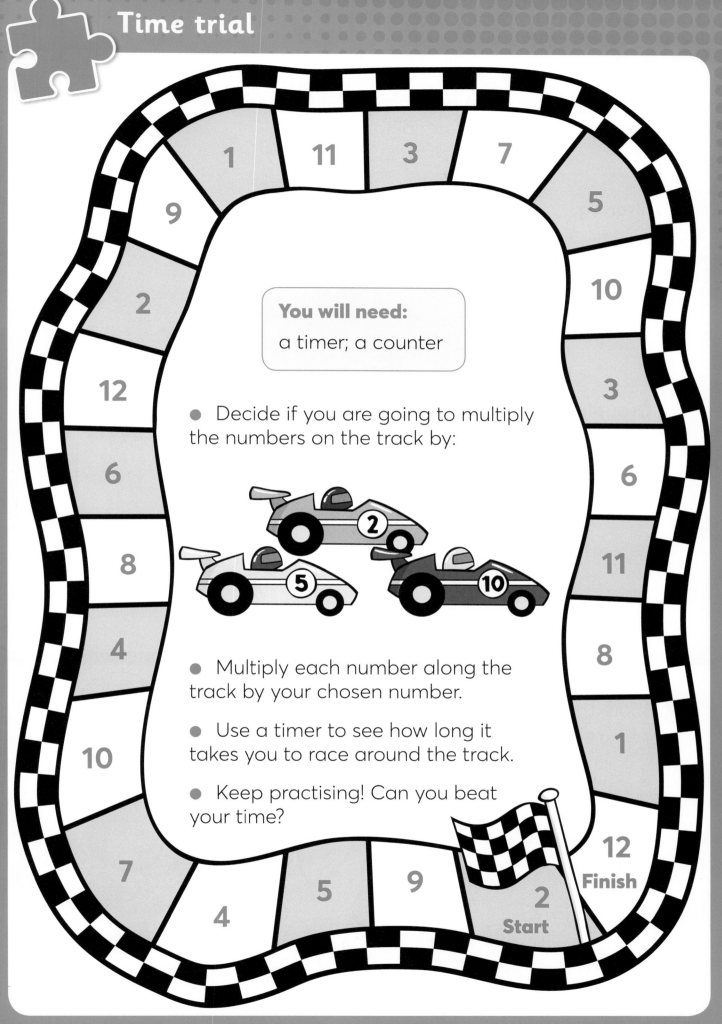

You will need:

a timer; a counter

● Decide if you are going to multiply the numbers on the track by:

● Multiply each number along the track by your chosen number.

● Use a timer to see how long it takes you to race around the track.

● Keep practising! Can you beat your time?

1 11 3 7

9

5

2

10

12

3

6

6

8

11

4

8

10

1

7

5 9

4

2
Start

12
Finish

You can split a number of objects into equal groups by sharing or grouping.

I have 12 sweets.

Sharing

I share the 12 sweets between 3 children.

Grouping

I can put 4 sweets in each bag.

There are 3 groups 4 of in 12.

 **1** Share the balloons equally between 2 children.

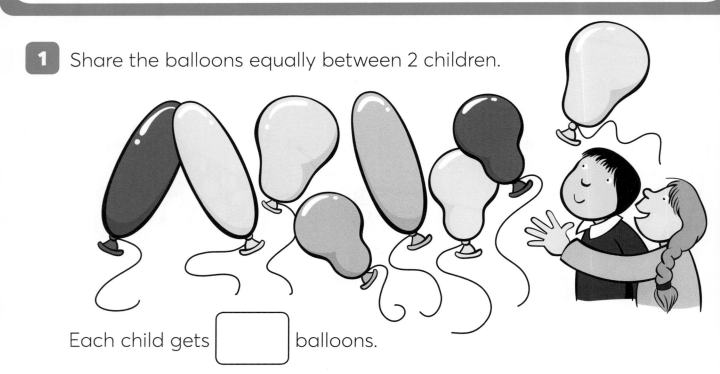

Each child gets ☐ balloons.

2 Draw circles around groups of 2 shoes to show the equal groups. One has been done for you.

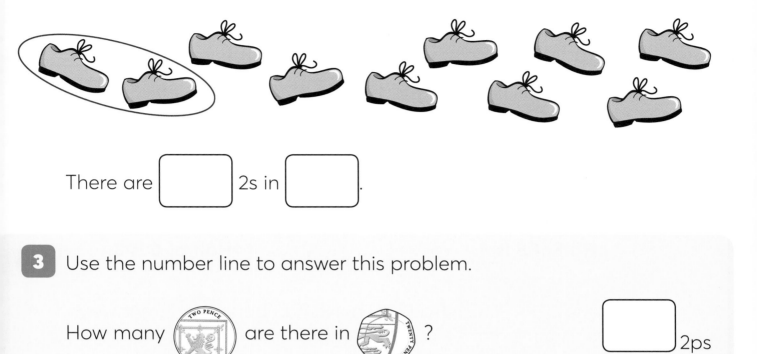

There are ⬚ 2s in ⬚.

3 Use the number line to answer this problem.

How many 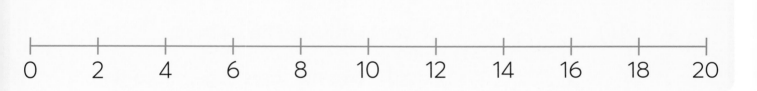 are there in ⬚ ? ⬚ 2ps

```
┬────┬────┬────┬────┬────┬────┬────┬────┬────┬────┬
0    2    4    6    8    10   12   14   16   18   20
```

4 Emilio has 20 flowers and some vases.

He puts 5 flowers in each vase. How many vases does he fill?

Draw a picture on a piece of paper to help you work out the answer.

He fills ⬚ vases with ⬚ flowers in each vase.

Take a big handful of raisins. How many different ways can you arrange the raisins into equal groups? Eat a few raisins. How many equal groups can you make now? Keep going until you have no raisins left.

14 Halving

Halving means splitting a shape or number into 2 equal parts.

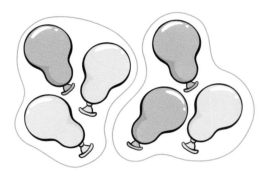

Half of 8 is 4.

Half of 6 is 3.

86	
80	6
40	3
43	

You can halve numbers in different ways.

First, separate the number into 10s and 1s.

Halve the 10s and halve the 1s.

Add the two numbers together to find the answer.

> A halving wall can help you halve larger numbers.

 1 Use doubles dominoes to help you work out these answers.

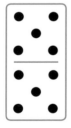 **a.** Half of 10 is ⬚

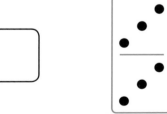 **c.** Half of 6 is ⬚

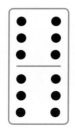 **b.** Half of 12 is ⬚

 **d.** Half of 8 is ⬚

2 Jasmine had 16p.

She spent half of it.

How much money did she have left?

Draw a picture to help you.

☐ p

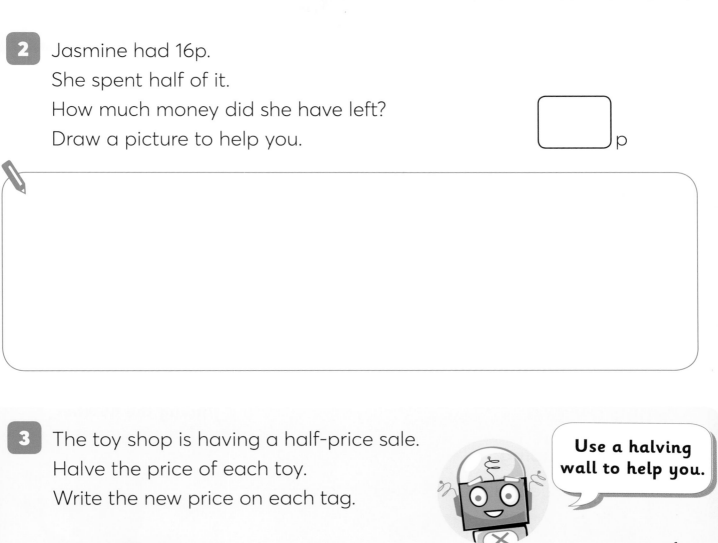

3 The toy shop is having a half-price sale.

Halve the price of each toy.

Write the new price on each tag.

Use a halving wall to help you.

Go outside and collect some pebbles. How many have you collected? Can you divide the number of pebbles in half or do you have 1 left over? Collect some leaves, pine cones or snail shells. Count them. Can you divide them in half?

15 Division

This sign ÷ means divided by.

Equal sharing

If I share 15 seeds equally between 5 pots, there will be 3 seeds in each pot.

15 shared between 5 is 3.

We can write this as a sentence using the division symbol ÷

15 ÷ 5 = 3

Equal grouping

I have 15 seeds. I plant 5 seeds in each pot.

There are 3 groups of 5 in 15. We can write this as a division sentence 15 ÷ 5 = 3.

> Division means sharing equally or finding the number of equal groups.

1 Share these 12 marbles equally into 4 groups. Draw the groups in the boxes below.

2 **a.** Circle the mice to show groups of 2. One has been done for you.

b. Write a number sentence to show the division.

There are ☐ 2s in 8.

☐ ÷ ☐ = ☐

3 Anna has 25 pencils to put into pots.
She puts 5 pencils in each pot.
How many pots does she fill?

☐ pots

Draw a picture on a separate piece of paper
to help you find the answer.

4 Answer each division. Use pebbles or pasta shells to help you.

a. 30 ÷ 5 = ☐

b. 50 ÷ 10 = ☐

c. 14 ÷ 2 = ☐

Use the toys in your bedroom to help you write your own division sentences. 6 soft toys grouped in 3s would be: 6 ÷ 3 = 2.

Multiplication is the opposite of division.

 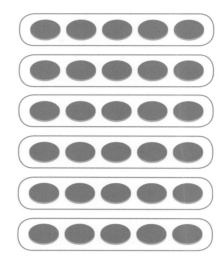

$6 \times 5 = 30$ $30 \div 5 = 6$

When you carry out a division you can check
your answer with a multiplication.

---

1 Write two multiplication and two division sentences to describe
this array.
Draw a ring around each row to group the dots.

 ☐ × ☐ = ☐    ☐ ÷ ☐ = ☐

☐ × ☐ = ☐   ☐ ÷ ☐ = ☐

2 Fill in the missing numbers by dividing by 2, 5 and 10.

a.

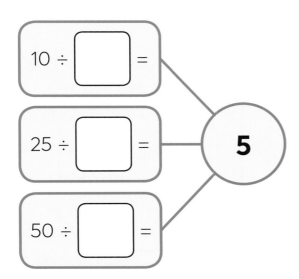

10 ÷ [ ] =

25 ÷ [ ] =

50 ÷ [ ] =

5

b.

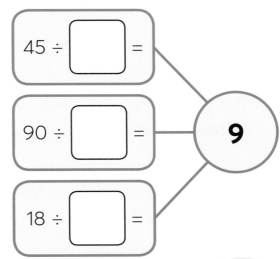

45 ÷ [ ] =

90 ÷ [ ] =

18 ÷ [ ] =

9

Remember you can use multiplication to check your answer is correct.

3 Answer these questions.

a. 90 ÷ 10 = [ ]   **b.** 30 ÷ 10 = [ ]   **c.** [ ] ÷ 10 = 2

How does knowing the 10-times table help you to divide by 10?
Talk about your ideas with an adult.

Now try this

On a piece of paper, make as many multiplication and division sentences as you can with these number cards.

| 3 | 5 | 30 | 10 | 50 | 2 | × | ÷ | = |

Help to sort the socks in the washing basket. Group socks into pairs to practise division facts for the 2 times table.

Crack the code

- The pirates have found an ancient treasure map.

- They need to crack the code to help them find the treasure.

- Help the pirates work out the answer to each multiplication and division sentence.

- Use the code to change the answers into letters and reveal where the treasure is buried.

a	d	f	g	i	k	l	m	n	o	p	s	t	u
18	7	5	3	6	9	4	11	2	10	16	14	8	12

1 × 5	12 ÷ 2	1 × 2	14 ÷ 2

15 ÷ 5	2 × 5	8 ÷ 2	70 ÷ 10

30 ÷ 3	20 ÷ 10

16 ÷ 2	100 ÷ 10	8 × 2

90 ÷ 9	50 ÷ 10

7 × 2	45 ÷ 5	24 ÷ 2	20 ÷ 5	2 × 2

110 ÷ 10	1 × 10	60 ÷ 5	10 ÷ 5	4 × 2	9 × 2	3 × 2	1 × 2

Double or halve it?

This is a game for 2 players.
You will need:
two 1–6 dice
several counters (of two different colours) for each player

- Take turns to roll both dice.

- Add the two numbers on the dice together.

- Decide whether to double or halve the total, then find the answer.

- Cover the number you have made with one of your counters.

- The winner is the first player to cover five numbers in a row.

1	16	8	22	6	14
18	2	22	8	16	3
10	20	3	4	10	18
4	24	5	20	6	12
12	1	5	14	24	2

Times tables tests

Have a go at the tests below, which test your knowledge of the 2-, 5- and 10-times tables.

Test 1
Multiplying by 2

a. 4 × 2 =

b. 6 × 2 =

c. 1 × 2 =

d. 9 × 2 =

e. 12 × 2 =

f. 10 × 2 =

g. 5 × 2 =

h. 3 × 2 =

Test 2
Multiplying by 5

a. 10 × 5 =

b. 8 × 5 =

c. 1 × 5 =

d. 6 × 5 =

e. 11 × 5 =

f. 2 × 5 =

g. 7 × 5 =

h. 9 × 5 =

Test 3
Multiplying by 10

a. 1 × 10 =

b. 10 × 10 =

c. 9 × 10 =

d. 3 × 10 =

e. 11 × 10 =

f. 8 × 10 =

g. 6 × 10 =

h. 4 × 10 =

Test 4 – Multiplying by 2, 5 and 10

a. 4 × 5 =

b. 8 × 2 =

c. 7 × 2 =

d. 5 × 10 =

e. 7 × 10 =

f. 12 × 10 =

g. 3 × 5 =

h. 2 × 2 =

Ask an adult to time you. Can you improve your time for each test?

Test 5
Multiplying and dividing by 2

a. 5 × 2 =

b. 20 ÷ 2 =

c. 8 ÷ 2 =

d. 22 ÷ 2 =

e. 4 × 2 =

f. 6 ÷ 2 =

g. 10 × 2 =

h. 8 × 2 =

Test 6
Multiplying and dividing by 5

a. 6 × 5 =

b. 15 ÷ 5 =

c. 35 ÷ 5 =

d. 45 ÷ 5 =

e. 12 × 5 =

f. 2 × 5 =

g. 10 ÷ 5 =

h. 50 ÷ 5 =

Test 7
Multiplying and dividing by 10

a. 30 ÷ 10 =

b. 2 × 10 =

c. 5 × 10 =

d. 90 ÷ 10 =

e. 70 ÷ 10 =

f. 7 × 10 =

g. 100 ÷ 10 =

h. 12 × 10 =

Test 8 – Multiplying and dividing by 2, 5 and 10

a. 20 ÷ 10 =

b. 5 ÷ 5 =

c. 3 × 5 =

d. 9 × 2 =

e. 4 × 5 =

f. 16 ÷ 2 =

g. 60 ÷ 5 =

h. 40 ÷ 10 =

Progress chart

Work through one unit at a time before moving on to the next one.

Making progress? Tick (✔) the circles as you complete each section of the book.

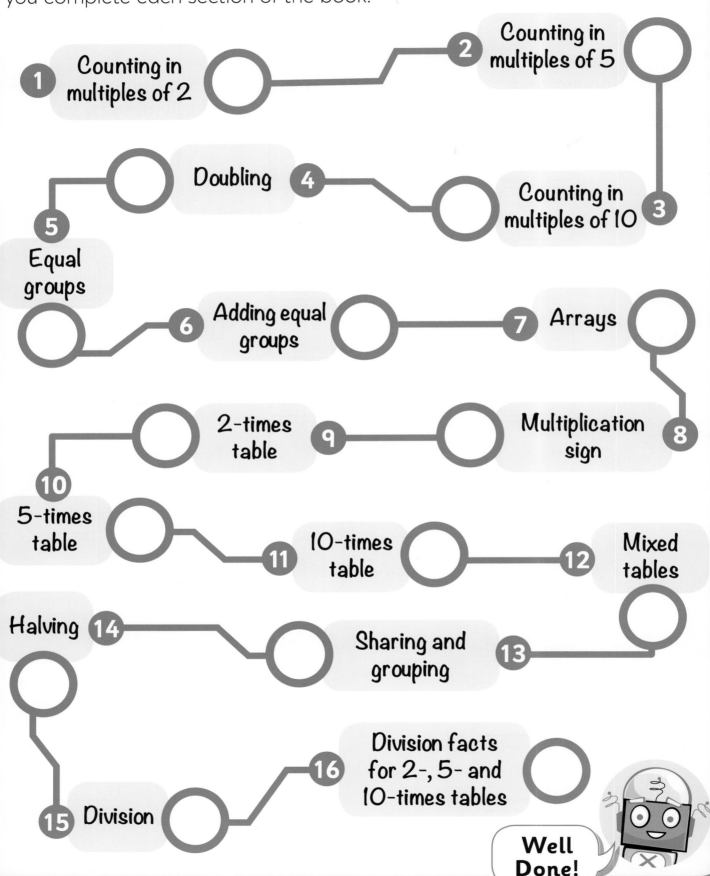

1 Counting in multiples of 2

2 Counting in multiples of 5

3 Counting in multiples of 10

4 Doubling

5 Equal groups

6 Adding equal groups

7 Arrays

8 Multiplication sign

9 2-times table

10 5-times table

11 10-times table

12 Mixed tables

13 Sharing and grouping

14 Halving

15 Division

16 Division facts for 2-, 5- and 10-times tables

Well Done!

Answers

Unit	Question number	Answers
1 Counting in multiples of 2 pages 6–7	1	a. b. 12 stars
	2	2 4 6 **8** **10**
	3	a. 12 **10** 8 **6** 4 2 b. All the numbers are even. They go down in 2s in a sequence.
	4	14 earrings
2 Counting in multiples of 5 pages 8–9	1	The shaded numbers are arranged in two columns. The numbers all end in 5 or 0.
	2	35 gold coins
	3	a. 15 20 **25 30** 35 **40** b. 30 **25** 20 **15** 10 **5**
	4	30 metres
	5	All the numbers end in 5 or 0. If I add 5 to a number that ends in 5, the answer always ends in a 0. If I add 5 to a number that ends in 0, the answer always ends in 5.
3 Counting in multiples of 10 pages 10–11	1	a. 70 legs b. 50 legs c. 30 legs
	2	a. 30 points, 70 points, 50 points, 60 points b. The top score is 100 points. Each child throws 10 rings. If all 10 rings land on the post, 100 is scored. 10 lots of 10 = 100.
	3	a. **30** 40 **50** 60 **70** b. 100 **90** 80 **70** 60
	4	a. 50p b. 80p
4 Doubling pages 12–13	1	
	2	3 + 3 = 6 2 + 2 = 4 5 + 5 = 10

Unit	Question number	Answers
4 Doubling pages 12–13	3	
	4	a. 8 sides b. 16 years old
	5	The answer is not an odd number. When you double an odd number the answer is always even, for example double 7 is 14, double 11 is 22. If you double an even number the answer will always be even. For example, double 4 is 8, double 12 is 24.
5 Equal groups pages 14–15	1	There are **4** equal groups with **5** in each group.
	2	
	3	
	4	
	5	a. a picture showing 6 equal groups of 2, for example b. a picture showing 7 equal groups of 5, for example
6 Adding equal groups pages 16–17	1	3 + 3 = 6 2 + 2 + 2 + 2 + 2 = 10 5 + 5 = 10
	2	3 + 3 = 6
	3	a. 15 seeds b. 0 3 6 9 12 15 20
	4	5 10ps because this is 50p. If you had 8 5ps, you would only have 40p and wouldn't have as much money to spend.

Unit	Question number	Answers
7 Arrays **pages 18–19**	1	a. 2 rows b. 5 cabbages c. 10 cabbages
	2	a. b. Rory planted the most carrots because 2 lots of 5 is 10. Amelia planted 8 carrots because 4 lots of 2 is 8.
	3	20 apples
	4	Children can make these arrays: 1 row of 10, 10 rows of 1, 5 rows of 2 and 2 rows of 5.
8 Multiplication sign **pages 20–21**	1	6 lots of 2 $6 \times 2 = 12$
	2	2 lots of 4
	3	$8 \times 5 = 40$
	4	$4 \times 10 = 40$, $10 \times 4 = 40$ The same numbers are multiplied together but in a different order. It gives the same answer no matter which order the numbers are in.
9 The 2-times table **pages 22–23**	1	a. $1 \times 2 = 2$ g. $7 \times 2 = \mathbf{14}$ b. $2 \times 2 = \mathbf{4}$ h. $8 \times 2 = \mathbf{16}$ c. $3 \times 2 = \mathbf{6}$ i. $9 \times 2 = \mathbf{18}$ d. $4 \times 2 = \mathbf{8}$ j. $10 \times 2 = \mathbf{20}$ e. $5 \times 2 = \mathbf{10}$ k. $11 \times 2 = \mathbf{22}$ f. $6 \times 2 = \mathbf{12}$ l. $12 \times 2 = \mathbf{24}$
	2	a. 14 worms b. 22 eggs
	3	All the numbers are even.
	4	Yes. If you multiply a number by 2 the answer is always even. This is because when you multiply a number by 2, you count in steps of 2 to find the answer. Multiples of 2 are always even.

Unit	Question number	Answers
10 The 5-times table **pages 24–25**	1	a. $8 \times 5 = 40$ b. $5 \times 5 = 25$
	2	55 stickers
	3	
	4	40 straws
	5	The statement is **sometimes** correct. If you multiply an even number by 5 the answer will always end in 0, for example $4 \times 5 = 20$, $8 \times 5 = 40$ but if you multiply an odd number by 5 the answer will always end in 5 for example $5 \times 5 = 25$, $1 \times 5 = 5$.
11 The 10-times table **pages 26–27**	1	
	2	a. $\mathbf{4} \times 10 = 40$ b. $\mathbf{6} \times 10 = 60$ c. $\mathbf{11} \times 10 = 110$
	3	70 potatoes
	4	a. 5 packs b. 6 balloons 4 packs (40 balloons) are not enough. 5 packs (50 balloons) are too many so there would be 6 left over.

Unit	Question number	Answers
12 Mixed tables pages 28–29	1	a. 30p b. 70p c. 20p
	2	(matching: 5 × 2 — 10 × 2; 8 × 5 — 4 × 10; 0 × 10 — 0 × 2; 3 × 10 — 6 × 5; 4 × 5 — 1 × 10)
	3	a. 8 × 10 = **80** d. **9** × 10 = 90 b. **5** × 10 = 50 e. **7** × 10 = 70 c. 1 × 10 = **10** f. 12 × 10 = **120**
	4	1 × 20 = 20 20 × 1 = 20 2 × 10 = 20 10 × 2 = 20 5 × 4 = 20 4 × 5 = 20
13 Sharing and grouping pages 32–33	1	Each child gets **4** balloons.
	2	a. b. There are **5** 2s in **10**.
	3	10 2ps
	4	Emilio fills **4** vases with **5** flowers in each vase.
14 Halving pages 34–35	1	a. Half of 10 is **5** c. Half of 6 is **3** b. Half of 12 is **6** d. Half of 8 is **4**
	2	8p
	3	
15 Division pages 36–37	1	
	2	 There are **4** 2s in 8. **8** ÷ **2** = **4**
	3	**5** pots

Unit	Question number	Answers
15 Division pages 36–37	4	a. 30 ÷ 5 = **6** b. 50 ÷ 10 = **5** c. 14 ÷ 2 = **7**
16 Division facts for 2-, 5- and 10-times tables pages 38–39	1	3 × 10 = 30 30 ÷ 10 = 3 10 × 3 = 30 30 ÷ 3 = 10
	2	a. (10 ÷ **2** =, 25 ÷ **5** =, 50 ÷ **10** = → 5) b. (45 ÷ **5** =, 90 ÷ **10** =, 18 ÷ **2** = → 9)
	3	a. 90 ÷ 10 = **9** b. 30 ÷ 10 = **3** c. 20 ÷ 10 = 2 Division is the opposite of multiplication. If you try to work out 90 ÷ 10 you can use your knowledge of the ten times table to help you. You know that 9 × 10 = 90 so 90 ÷ 10 must be 9.
Game: Crack the code		The code is: find gold on top of skull mountain

Unit	Question number	Answers			
Times tables tests: 2, 5, 10 page 42	**Test 1** Multiplying by 2	a. 8 b. 12	c. 2 d. 18	e. 24 f. 20	g. 10 h. 6
	Test 2 Multiplying by 5	a. 50 b. 40	c. 5 d. 30	e. 55 f. 10	g. 35 h. 45
	Test 3 Multiplying by 10	a. 10 b. 100	c. 90 d. 30	e. 110 f. 80	g. 60 h. 40
	Test 4 Multiplying by 2, 5 and 10	a. 20 b. 16	c. 14 d. 50	e. 70 f. 120	g. 15 h. 4
Times tables tests: 2, 5, 10 page 43	**Test 5** Multiplying and dividing by 2	a. 10 b. 10	c. 4 d. 11	e. 8 f. 3	g. 20 h. 16
	Test 6 Multiplying and dividing by 5	a. 30 b. 3	c. 7 d. 9	e. 60 f. 10	g. 2 h. 10
	Test 7 Multiplying and dividing by 10	a. 3 b. 20	c. 50 d. 9	e. 7 f. 70	g. 10 h. 120
	Test 8 Multiplying and dividing by 2, 5, and 10	a. 2 b. 1	c. 15 d. 18	e. 20 f. 8	g. 12 h. 4

QUICK TESTS FOR SATs SUCCESS

BOOST YOUR CHILD'S CONFIDENCE WITH 10-MINUTE SATs TESTS

- Bite-size mini SATs tests which take just 10 minutes to complete
- Covers key National Test topics
- Full answers and progress chart provided to track improvement
- Available for Years 1 to 6

Find out more at www.scholastic.co.uk